ALOHA! Greetings!

Library of Congress Catalogue No. 75-27131
Book Design: Barbara Bradley
Recipes and Text: Patricia Collier, Castle & Cooke Foods
Dole, Bumble Bee, Hawaiian Kids Registered Trademarks
of Castle & Cooke, Inc.

Hawaiian Kids™
COOKBOOK

QUICK AND EASY

RECIPES

FOR CHILDREN EVERYWHERE

PICTURES BY
BARBARA BRADLEY

Published by Recorder Publishing Co., San Francisco.   Copyright © 1975 by Castle & Cooke, Inc., Honolulu, Hawaii.   All rights reserved throughout the world.

In the Hawaiian alphabet there are only 12 letters:

A-"ah" - as in father   E-"ay" - as in obey
i-"ee" - as in caprice   O-"oh" - as in bold
U-"oo" - as in moon

H, K, L, M, N, P, W, are pronounced as in English.

CONTENTS

WORDS YOU SHOULD KNOW
BEFORE YOU START COOKING:

BAKE: Cook in the oven.

BOIL: Cook in hot liquid that bubbles and steams a lot. 1

BROIL: Cook very close to the heat; use the broiler in the oven or cook outside over coals.

FRY: Cook in hot fat, using a skillet. 2

SIMMER: Cook in liquid that bubbles and steams a little, over low heat. 3

PREHEAT: Heat oven before putting food in it.

BEAT: Mix fast with large spoon or electric mixer.

BLEND: Stir several ingredients together until the mixture is fairly smooth. 4

CREAM: Beat shortening first until it's smooth. Add sugar and keep beating until the mixture is light and fluffy.

FOLD: Mix gently using a spatula or a spoon. Cut down through the mixture, across the bottom and up over the top. Do this with a gentle hand, over and over, until the ingredients are well mixed. Do not beat. 5

MIX: Stir ingredients together thoroughly with a spoon or electric mixer.

WHIP: Beat very fast using an electric mixer or wire whip.

CHOP: Cut in small pieces. 6

CHUNK: Cut in large pieces.

4

5

6

DICE: Cut in small, even, usually square-shaped pieces. 7

7

SLICE: Cut in thin pieces. 8

CRUMBLE: Break up with your fingers.

8

MASH: Crush or smash food to a soft, fairly smooth mixture. 9

DOT: Scatter bits of butter or cheese over the top of food.

9

DRAIN: Pour off liquid from food, using a strainer or colander. 10

GREASE: Spread the bottom and sides of a pan with a thin layer of margarine or shortening.

CHILL: Making food cold, but not frozen.

10

BEST WAYS TO MEASURE:

DRY INGREDIENTS: Use metal or plastic measuring cups, fill to the top and level off with the flat side of a knife.

LIQUID INGREDIENTS: Use glass measuring cups. Have your eyes at the same level as the mark on the cup.

SHORTENING, PEANUT BUTTER & OTHER THICK INGREDIENTS: Pack into metal or plastic measuring cups a little at a time, pressing air out. Level off the top; then scrape out with a rubber scraper.

SMALL AMOUNTS: Use standard measuring spoons, not ones you use for meals. Level off the spoonful.

GOOD HABITS TO GET INTO:

1. Wash your hands first.

2. Put on an apron.

3. Read through the whole recipe and picture yourself doing it. Set out all the ingredients and utensils that you'll need so that you can work smoothly when you start.

4. Ask someone who knows if they will teach you how to use the oven, the range or any other equipment you may be using.

5. Work through the recipe one step at at time, following the directions carefully.

6. When you use a knife or vegetable peeler, cut away from yourself so there's less chance of cutting yourself.

7. When you open a can, tip the lid to one side by pressing down on the other side. Don't hold the sharp lid by the edges.

8. When you're finished with the recipe, clean up the kitchen, wash the dishes and put them away, and put away all extra ingredients.

9. If you used the oven or range, check to make sure it's off.

1

2

3

4

5

6

7

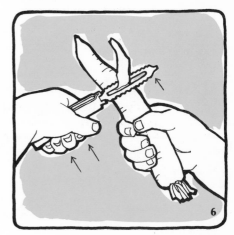

8

9

FEELING GREAT:

Eating good-for-you foods gives your body the fuel it needs to go, grow and make repairs. In return for giving it the proper fuel, your body lets you feel better and happier. The four important groups of food that a healthy body needs are:

1. Meats, poultry, fish, eggs & peanut butter
2. Milk, cheese, and dairy products
3. Breads, rice, potatoes, and cereal
4. Fruits, fruit juices, and vegetables

When you include some of each group in every meal (breakfast, lunch and dinner), your body will be getting all the nutrients it needs to stay in top running form. And you'll be feeling great.

TILLIE'S TUNA BITES

2 cans (6½ oz. each) Bumble Bee
    Chunk Light Tuna
4 ounces cream cheese, softened
1 ounce blue cheese, crumbled
2 tablespoons green onion, minced
¾ cup parsley
    Cherry tomatoes

1. Open tuna with a can opener; hold lid on tightly and drain off liquid over the sink. Empty tuna into a mixing bowl.
2. Stir in cream cheese and blue cheese until they are smooth and creamy.
3. Stir in green onions. Put a piece of plastic wrap over bowl and put in refrigerator for 1 hour.
4. Chop parsley on a board until it is very fine. Put in a shallow pan.
5. Using a teaspoon, make small balls of the tuna mixture.
6. Roll the balls in the chopped parsley. Put them on a flat plate.
7. Place the cherry tomatoes around the balls to decorate. Makes 3 dozen appetizers.

tuna
  'ahi

conch shell
  pū

onion
  'aka'akai

eat
  'ai

Dennis
  Kenika

generous
  manawale'a

blow
  puhi, pā

HAM 'N CHEESE DUNK

½ cup cheese spread
½ cup dairy sour cream
½ teaspoon dill weed
3 large Dole Bananas
2 cups cooked ham chunks
Toothpicks

1. If cheese spread is cold, let it stand at room temperature 1 hour.
2. Measure sour cream, cheese spread and dill weed into a medium-size bowl. Stir with a wire whip until smooth.
3. Pour into a small bowl to serve.
4. Peel bananas and cut into ½-inch slices.
5. Cut ham into chunks about ½-inch square.
6. Stick one ham chunk and one banana slice on each toothpick. Arrange picks on a plate.
7. Serve with cheese dunk. Makes 3 dozen.

David
Kāwika

Ann, Anna
Ana

jump, leap, fly
lele

look
nānā

pool
ki'o wai

water
wai

appetizer
pupu

DEEP SEA DIP

4 strips bacon
1 can (6½ oz.) Bumble Bee
   Chunk Light Tuna
½ cup cottage cheese
⅓ cup minced onion
1 can (2 oz.) sliced pimiento
¾ cup dairy sour cream
   Potato or corn chips

1. In a medium-size fry pan, fry bacon over medium heat until crisp, turning once. Drain on paper towels.
2. Open tuna with a can opener; hold lid on tightly and drain off liquid over the sink. Empty tuna into a mixing bowl.
3. Break up large pieces of tuna with a fork. Add cottage cheese, minced onion, pimiento and sour cream, mixing well.
4. Crumble bacon into small bits with fingers; add to dip.
5. Spoon mixture into a serving bowl and serve with potato chips or corn chips. Makes 2 cups dip.

three
ekolu

Thomas
Koma

waterfall
wailele

cottage cheese
waiūhakuhaku

whee!, oh!
auwē!

dinner
'aina

slide
pakika

PICNIC TUNA PUPS

1 can (6½ oz.) Bumble Bee
   Chunk Light Tuna
   Mayonnaise
4 hot dog buns
12 sweet pickle chips
½ tomato

1. Open tuna with can opener. Hold lid on tightly and drain off liquid over sink.
2. In a small bowl, combine tuna with about 3 tablespoons mayonnaise. Break up large chunks of tuna with fork as you mix.
3. Spread tuna mixture on one side of each hot dog bun. Spread mayonnaise on other side. Place pickle chips on top of tuna.
4. Slice tomato thinly and arrange slices on pickle. Gently squeeze bun so sandwich holds together. Makes 4 servings.

Emily
Emelē

bird
manu

beach
kahakai

sand
one (oh-ney)

sarong
pā'ū

feather
hulu

again
hou

CLUB HOUSE SPECIAL

1 pkg. (8 oz.) cream cheese
1 can (6½ oz.) Bumble Bee Chunk
   Light Tuna
½ cup minced celery
1 green onion minced
2 tablespoons pickle relish
2 dozen assorted crackers

1. Let cream cheese stand at room temperature for at least 1 hour to soften.
2. Open tuna with a can opener; hold lid on tightly and drain off liquid over the sink.
3. In a medium-size mixer bowl, beat cream cheese until it is fluffy. Remove beater.
4. Add tuna to cream cheese, breaking up large sections with a fork. Stir well.
5. Add minced celery, green onion and pickle relish, blending well.
6. With a table knife, spread a little tuna spread on each cracker. Arrange crackers on a serving plate and carry out to your club house—or wherever your special club meeting is being held! Makes 2 dozen.

NOTE: These may be made ahead of time, covered with plastic wrap and kept in the refrigerator until your meeting adjourns for refreshments.

Frank
Palani

drum
pahu

celery
kelaki

club
hui

over
pau

leader
alakai

reward
makana

23

TUNA TURNOVERS

1 can (6½ oz.) Bumble Bee
    Chunk Light Tuna
¼ cup chopped celery
¼ cup chopped green onion
¼ cup mayonnaise

1 tablespoon lemon juice
1 package (8 oz.) refrigerated
    crescent rolls
3 slices American cheese

1. Turn oven on to 375° F.
2. Open tuna with can opener. Hold lid on tightly and drain off liquid over the sink. Put tuna in a medium-size mixing bowl.
3. Chop celery and onion; add to tuna along with mayonnaise and lemon juice.
4. Open crescent roll dough. Separate the two sections and spread one out on waxed paper. Gently pinch the separation places together to make one long rectangle of dough. Then cut with a knife into 3 squares. Repeat with second section of dough.
5. Divide tuna mixture evenly and spread gently on each square. Keep tuna near center of dough.
6. Fold each square in half diagonally to make triangles. Press edges together with a fork to close turnover.
7. Carefully place turnovers on a baking sheet. Bake in oven for about 10 minutes.
8. Cut cheese slices in half diagonally to make triangles. With potholders, carefully remove baking sheet from oven. Place one piece of cheese on each turnover. Return baking sheet to oven and bake about 1 minute longer, until cheese melts.
9. With potholders, remove baking sheet from oven. Turn oven off. Serve turnovers warm. Makes 6 servings.

Robert
Lopaka

Sarah
Kala

to bake
kālua

one
akāhi

lemon
lemi

more
hou

service
hana

How many?
'Ehia?

25

SATURDAY SANDWICH

1 can (6½ oz.) Bumble Bee
   Chunk Light Tuna
1 stalk celery
1 sweet pickle
1 green onion
¼ cup dairy sour cream
1 large Dole Banana
2 teaspoons lemon juice
8 slices wheat bread

1. Open tuna with a can opener; hold lid on tightly and drain off liquid into sink.
2. Place tuna in a medium-size bowl and break up with a fork.
3. Cut celery into ¼-inch slices. Chop pickle and green onion into small pieces. Add celery, pickle and green onion to tuna.
4. Measure sour cream into bowl; stir in with spoon.
5. Peel banana; chop into small pieces.
6. In a separate small bowl, mix banana pieces with lemon juice; then add to tuna and stir in gently.
7. Divide mixture between 4 slices of bread. Spread evenly on bread.
8. Top with second slices. Makes 4 sandwiches.

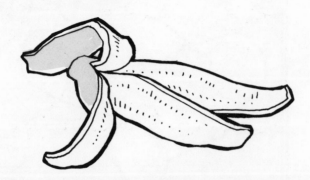

Saturday
Pōaōno

school
kula

bread
palaoa

Mark
Maleko

carry
lawe

stomach
ōpū

mix
kāwili

BACON, LETTUCE AND BANANA SANDWICHES

6 slices bacon
2 tablespoons mayonnaise
4 slices white bread
2 lettuce leaves
1 large Dole Banana

1. Cook bacon in a heavy frying pan over medium heat. Turn over once and cook until crisp. Lift to paper towels to drain. Turn heat off.
2. Spread mayonnaise on 2 slices bread.
3. Arrange lettuce on mayonnaise.
4. Peel banana and cut into ½-inch slices; place slices on lettuce.
5. Top with cooked bacon and second slices of bread. Makes 2 sandwiches.

Alice
Aleka

lettuce
lekuke

flower necklace
lei

silly (crazy)
pupule

bird's eye view
ki'i maka manu

hold
paa

branch
lālā

29

T-P-T SANDWICH

1 can (8¼ oz.) Dole Sliced
   Pineapple in Juice
4 slices dark or white bread
¼ cup mayonnaise
4 slices cooked turkey or ham
1 tomato
4 slices cheddar or Monterey
   Jack cheese

1. Turn oven on to 400° F.
2. Open pineapple with can opener. Hold lid on tightly and drain off liquid over the sink.
3. Arrange bread on a baking sheet. Divide mayonnaise evenly and spread on bread.
4. Place one turkey or ham slice on each piece of bread.
5. Slice tomato and place a slice in center of each sandwich.
6. Cut pineapple slices in half and arrange halves on either side of tomato.
7. Top each sandwich with a slice of cheese.
8. Place in oven and bake for 10 minutes. Remove with potholders. Turn oven off.
Makes 4 servings.

Paul
Paulo

standard of royalty
kāhili

hungry
pōloli

yellow
melemele

grass
mauu

breeze
aheahe makani

cheese
waiūpakapaʻa

carrying
hapaina

CONFETTI SANDWICH

1 can (6½ oz.) Bumble Bee Chunk
    Light Tuna
⅓ cup sliced black olives
¼ cup minced red onion
⅓ cup mayonnaise
4 slices bread
¼ cup minced green pepper
1 cup shredded cheddar cheese

1. Open tuna with can opener; hold lid on tightly and drain off liquid over the sink. Empty tuna into a small mixing bowl. Break up large chunks of tuna with a fork.
2. Slice olives and mince onion, add to tuna.
3. Measure mayonnaise; add half to the tuna mixture. Blend well.
4. Spread tuna mixture on bread, dividing evenly.
5. Mince green pepper.
6. In a small bowl, combine shredded cheese, green pepper and mayonnaise, blending well.
7. Divide among sandwiches and spread carefully on top of tuna.
8. Place sandwiches on a broiler pan. Put in oven; turn on broiler and cook for about 7 minutes.
9. Remove pan from oven carefully with potholders. Turn oven off. Makes 4 servings.

Katherine
Kakalina

flowers
pua

greetings everyone
aloha kakou

come and eat
hele mai ai

meal
'aina

toss
hoolei

bowl
'umeke

ALL-TIME GREATEST SANDWICH

3 tablespoons peanut butter
4 slices white bread
1 large Dole Banana

1. Spread peanut butter on two slices of bread.
2. Peel banana and cut into ¼-inch slices. Arrange banana slices on peanut butter.
3. Top with second slices of bread. Makes 2 sandwiches.

NOTE: If you want to make it special, you can add honey, lettuce, bacon or shredded cheddar cheese to your sandwiches.

King Kamehameha - *Great ruler of Hawaii many years ago*

Andrew
Analū

Susie
Kuke

first
mua

orange
alani

butter
waiūpaka

feast
lūau

palace
hale alii

FANCY HAM & CHEESE

4 slices rye, wheat or
   pumpernickel bread
2 tablespoons mayonnaise
2 thick slices ham
2 slices Jack or Cheddar cheese
1 large Dole Banana
   Lettuce

1. Spread bread slices with mayonnaise.
2. Place one slice ham and one slice cheese on each of 2 slices bread.
3. Peel banana, and cut into ¼-inch slices. Arrange banana slices on cheese.
4. Top with lettuce and second slices of bread. Makes 2 sandwiches.

Becky
Peke

covered with leis
'ohu 'ohu

nice
'auli'i

okay
hiki

smart
akamai

strong
ikaika

gift
makana

BOTTOMS UP BISCUITS

2 tablespoons butter
¼ cup brown sugar, firmly packed
⅓ cup pecan halves
¼ cup flaked coconut
1 large Dole Banana
1 package (8 oz.) refrigerated
    buttermilk biscuits

1. Turn oven on to 450° F.
2. Place butter in an 8-inch round cake pan; heat over low heat until butter melts.
3. With potholders, remove from heat. Stir in brown sugar with a spoon.
4. Arrange pecan halves in the pan; sprinkle with coconut.
5. Peel banana and chop into small pieces. Drop banana on coconut.
6. Open biscuit dough and separate it into 10 pieces. Lightly press biscuits on mixture in cake pan.
7. Place pan in oven. Bake about 10 minutes, until browned.
8. With potholders, remove cake pan from oven and run a table knife around edge of pan to loosen biscuits.
9. Immediately turn upside down on serving plate. Let pan remain on biscuits one minute before removing pan.
10. Turn off oven. Serve biscuits warm. Makes 10 biscuits.

Barbara
Palapala

Bottoms up!
Ōkole maluna!

pretty
nani

life, health
ola

wet
pulu

to swim
ʻau

dolphin
mahimahi

39

ISLAND NUT BREAD

3 cups flour
1 cup sugar
4 teaspoons baking powder
1 teaspoon salt
1 can (8¼ oz.) Dole Crushed
    Pineapple

1¼ cups buttermilk
1 egg
¼ cup butter
½ cup Royal Hawaiian Bits O'
    Macadamia Nuts, or
    chopped pecans

1. Turn oven on to 350° F.
2. In a large mixing bowl, combine flour, sugar, baking powder and salt.
3. Open pineapple with a can opener and pour it into another bowl. Add buttermilk and egg, mixing well.
4. In a small saucepan, over medium heat, melt butter. Add to pineapple mixture.
5. Pour all the pineapple mixture into the flour mixture. Stir with a spoon until it is well mixed.
6. Stir in nuts.
7. Grease an 8-inch loaf pan with a little shortening. Pour in batter.
8. Bake in oven for about 1 hour.
9. Carefully remove bread from oven with potholders. Let it cool for about 10 minutes. Then remove from pan.
10. Turn oven off. Makes 1 loaf.

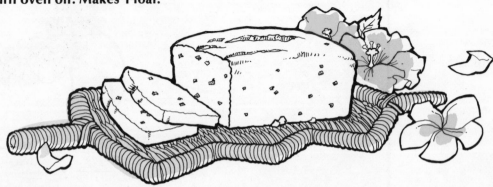

James, Jim
Kimo

Helen
Helena

sugar
kōpaa

drop
kulu

lie down, sleep
hiamoe

salt
pa'akai

mouth
waha

POT O' GOLD MUFFINS

1 cup corn meal
1 cup flour
2 teaspoons baking powder
1 teaspoon salt
⅓ cup butter, softened
2 tablespoons chopped chives

1 can (8¼ oz.) Dole Crushed
    Pineapple
1 egg
½ cup milk
12 chunks (½-inch each)
    cheddar cheese

1. Turn oven on to 400°F.
2. Combine corn meal, flour, baking powder and salt in a mixing bowl.
3. Ask someone who knows to help you "cut in" the softened butter. Then add chives.
4. Open pineapple with a can opener. Pour pineapple and all the syrup into corn meal mixture.
5. Add egg and milk to corn meal and stir all together until mixed.
6. Line 12 muffin cups with paper liners.
7. Place one spoonful of batter in each cup. Place a chunk of cheese in center of each cup. Cover cheese with another spoonful of batter, dividing evenly.
8. Place in oven and bake for 25 minutes, until browned. With potholders, remove muffins from oven. Turn oven off.
9. Let muffins cool about 10 minutes before handling them. Serve warm. Makes 1 dozen.

Mary
Malia

Michael
Mika'ele

paddle
hoe

ocean
moana

sea water
kai

egg
hua

TROPICAL SHAKE

1 can (8¼ oz.) Dole Crushed
    Pineapple
¾ cup milk
2 large scoops vanilla ice cream
¼ cup light corn syrup
1 teaspoon vanilla extract

1. Open pineapple with can opener. Add pineapple and all syrup to blender jar.
2. Measure all the other ingredients into the blender jar.
3. Cover with lid and turn blender on to medium speed. Wait 10 seconds; then turn blender off.
4. Pour milk shake into 2 tall glasses. Makes 2 servings.

The Beauty
Nani

pineapple
hala-kahiki

ice cream
haukalime

shake
ho'oluli

blue (clothes, eyes)
polū

blue (of deep sea)
uli

taste
hoāo

QUICK-AS-A-WINK BREAKFAST DRINK

1½ cups milk
1 large Dole Banana
¼ cup honey
1 egg
¼ teaspoon cinnamon
2 tablespoons wheat germ

1. Measure milk into blender jar.
2. Peel banana; break it into 3 or four pieces and add to milk.
3. Measure honey, egg, cinnamon and wheat germ into blender jar.
4. Cover with lid and blend at highest speed until smooth. Pour into tall glasses.
   Makes 2 servings.

NOTE: You could add ice cream to make it special.

quick
'āwīwī

Nancy
Naneki

Peter
Pekelo

morning
kakahiaka

surfer
he'e nalu

sister
kaikuahine

hide
hūnā

behind
mahope

PICK-ME-UP PUNCH

1 can (46 oz.) Dole Pineapple
    Juice
3 cups apricot nectar
1 can (6 oz.) frozen lemonade
    concentrate
  Ice

1. Shake pineapple juice; open can and pour into a large pitcher.
2. Add apricot nectar and lemonade, stirring until lemonade dissolves.
3. Fill glasses with ice. Pour punch over ice to serve. Makes about 10 servings.

Kenneth
Keneke

Carol
Kalola

rain
ua

thunder
hekili

fruit
hua

catch
hopu

hear
lohe

brother
kaikunane

WAKE-UP BREAKFAST

1 can (8¼ oz.) Dole Crushed
    Pineapple
1 egg
1 cup milk
2 tablespoons honey or molasses
2 tablespoons nonfat dry milk
  Pinch salt

1. Open pineapple with can opener. Add pineapple and all syrup to blender jar.
2. Measure all the other ingredients into blender jar.
3. Cover with lid and turn blender on to high speed. Wait 30 seconds; then turn blender off.
4. Pour into 2 glasses. Makes 2 servings.

Patricia
Pakelekia

yoo-hoo
hui

pay
uku

sky
lani

rascal
kolohe

milk
waiū

dream
moeuhane

51

EGGNOG SMOOTHIE

1 cup milk
1 egg
1 large Dole Banana
⅛ teaspoon nutmeg
1 tablespoon sugar
Pinch salt

1. Measure milk and egg into blender jar.
2. Peel banana and break into 3 or 4 pieces. Add to blender.
3. Measure nutmeg, sugar and salt into blender.
4. Cover with lid and blend at highest speed until smooth.
5. Pour into tall glasses. Makes 2 servings.

Claire
Kalea

egg
hua

hand
lima

face
helehelena

flatter
hoomalimali

dance
hula

friend
hoaloha

CREAMY BANANA MILKSHAKE

2 scoops vanilla ice cream
1 cup milk
½ teaspoon vanilla extract
2 large Dole bananas

1. With an ice-cream scoop, place 2 scoops ice cream into blender jar.
2. Measure milk and vanilla into blender.
3. Peel bananas and break into 3 or 4 pieces. Add to blender.
4. Cover with lid and blend at highest speed until smooth.
5. Pour into tall glasses to serve. Makes 2 large servings.

NOTE: You can use chocolate or maple-nut ice cream, instead of vanilla, if you want to.

George
Keoki

finger
manamana lima

sloppy
kāpulu

child
keiki

ear
pepeiao

tongue
alelo

foot
wāwae

HOT CHOCOLATE DELUXE

2½ cups milk
1 large Dole Banana
3 tablespoons unsweetened cocoa
¼ cup sugar

1. Measure milk into blender jar.
2. Peel banana; break into 3 or 4 pieces and add to milk.
3. Measure cocoa and sugar into blender jar.
4. Cover with lid; blend at highest speed until smooth, about one minute.
5. Pour into a medium-size saucepan. Place over medium heat and stir slowly until cocoa is hot. This takes about 5 minutes. It should not boil.
6. Turn off heat. Serve in mugs or cups. Makes 4 servings.

Edward
Ekewaka

wave
nalu

hot
wela

Pacific
Pākīpika

to surf
he'e nalu

strong, powerful
ikaika

balance
koena

57

TUNA BELL SALAD

2 cans (7 oz. each) Bumble Bee
  Solid White Albacore Tuna
½ cup chopped celery
¼ cup chopped green onion
¼ cup sliced pimiento
½ cup dairy sour cream
3 large bell peppers

1. Open tuna with a can opener. Hold lid on tightly and drain liquid into the sink. Empty tuna into a medium-size mixing bowl. Break up large chunks of tuna with a fork.
2. Chop celery and green onion; add to tuna along with pimiento and sour cream. Mix all together well.
3. Cut bell peppers in half crosswise. Remove seeds and white insides with clean fingers. This will make 6 little containers.
4. Spoon tuna salad into bell peppers to serve. Makes 6 servings.

bell
pele

Geoffrey
Keopele

big
nui

to pull
huki

cream
kalima

cliff
pali

net
upena

59

SUMMER GARDEN SALAD

1   can (1 lb.) Bumble Bee
    Red Sockeye Salmon
½   medium-size cucumber
½   cup chopped green pepper
¼   cup minced red onion
⅓   cup dairy sour cream
½   teaspoon garlic salt
½   teaspoon dill weed
    Dash pepper
    Crisp lettuce

1. Open salmon with a can opener; hold lid on tightly and drain off liquid over sink. Empty salmon into a mixing bowl.
2. With clean fingers, remove large bones and skin from salmon. Break up large sections of fish.
3. Peel cucumber half with a vegetable peeler. Chop cucumber and green pepper. Mince onion. Add vegetables to salmon.
4. In a cup, stir together sour cream, garlic salt, dill weed and pepper. Pour over salmon and mix in gently.
5. Arrange lettuce on serving plates. Spoon salmon salad onto lettuce. Makes 4 servings.

Bill
Pila

Madeline
Makelina

summer
kau

garden
māla

enjoy
olioli

just for you
nāu wale no

play
pāani

TUNA TIKI SALAD

1 can (7 oz.) Bumble Bee Solid
    White Albacore Tuna
1 cup bean sprouts
⅓ cup chopped water chestnuts
⅓ cup chopped green onion
⅓ cup chopped radishes
2 tablespoons salad oil
2 tablespoons vinegar
1 tablespoon chopped parsley
¼ teaspoon garlic salt
    Crisp lettuce

1. Open tuna can with a can opener; hold lid on tightly and drain off liquid over the sink. Empty tuna into a medium-size mixing bowl.
2. Put bean sprouts in a large strainer. Rinse under cold water. Chop them coarsely with a knife. Add to tuna.
3. Chop water chestnuts, green onion and radishes. Add to tuna, mixing well.
4. Into a small cup, measure salad oil, vinegar, parsley and garlic salt. Stir together until well-blended. Pour over tuna salad, mixing well.
5. Arrange lettuce on serving plates. Spoon salad onto lettuce. Makes 4 servings.

Richard
Likeke

tiki
ki'i

crunch
kamumu

green
ōmaoma

teeth
niho

carve
kālai

wood
wahie

BANANA SPLIT SALAD

2 large Dole Bananas
1 cup cottage cheese
1 can (8 oz.) Dole Crushed
    Pineapple in Juice
2 maraschino cherries with stems

1. Peel bananas; carefully slice them in half lengthwise. Place two halves in each banana-split dish.
2. Using small ice cream scoop, place two scoops cottage cheese between banana halves for each salad.
3. Open pineapple with a can opener.
4. Spoon crushed pineapple and juice over cottage cheese.
5. Top each salad with a maraschino cherry. Makes 2 salads.

banana
mai'a

Amy
Eme

Steven
Kiwini

ginger blossom
awapuhi

girl
kaikamahine

shoulder
poohiwi

enough
lawa

TWO-TONE FRUIT MOLD

1 pkg. (6 oz.) strawberry
    gelatin mix
1½ cups boiling water
1 can (1 lb. 4 oz.) Dole Chunk
    Pineapple in Juice
1 carton (8 oz.) strawberry
    yogurt

1. Open gelatin package and pour into a medium-size mixing bowl.
2. Carefully add boiling water and stir with a spoon until gelatin dissolves.
3. Open pineapple with a can opener. Hold a large strainer over a cup and pour in pineapple. Let all the juice drain into the cup. Add all the juice to the gelatin along with ½ cup of cold water.
4. Carefully pour half the gelatin mixture into a 1½ quart ring mold. Place about half the pineapple chunks in the gelatin in an even pattern. Place ring mold in refrigerator and chill until firm.
5. To the rest of the gelatin mixture in the bowl, add strawberry yogurt. Stir gently with a wire whip until the yogurt is all mixed in. Add the rest of the chunk pineapple.
6. When gelatin is set in the ring mold, remove from refrigerator. Pour yogurt-gelatin mixture on top and put back in refrigerator. Chill at least 3 hours.
7. When ready to serve, run a table knife around the edge of the mold. Turn upside down over a plate and shake gently. The gelatin should come out evenly. Makes 6 to 8 servings.

Diana
Kiana

walk
hele

three
ekolu

basket
hina'i

red
ulaula

cold
anu

grow
ulu

TREASURE ISLAND SALAD

1 can (1 lb. 4 oz.) Dole Chunk
    Pineapple in Juice
1 cup sliced celery
½ cup pecan halves
½ cup chopped dates
⅓ cup mayonnaise
    Crisp lettuce

1. Open pineapple with can opener. Hold large strainer over bowl; empty can into strainer and let juice drain off. Drink juice.
2. In a medium-size mixing bowl, combine drained pineapple with all other ingredients except lettuce.
3. Spoon salad onto lettuce. Makes 4 to 6 servings.

Laura
  Lala

everything
  na mea a pau

thank you
  mahalo

open
  wehe

choose
  koho

island
  mokupuni

birthday
  lā hānau

RAINBOW FRUIT SALAD

1 can (1 lb. 4 oz.) Dole Chunk
 Pineapple in Juice
2 Dole Bananas
1 cup strawberries
1 cup grapes
1 cup blueberries
¼ cup coconut syrup, or honey

1. Open pineapple with can opener. Hold a large strainer over a cup or bowl and pour in pineapple. Let all the juice drain into the cup; reserve juice.
2. Put drained chunk pineapple into a large mixing bowl.
3. Peel banana; cut in ½-inch slices and add to pineapple.
4. Rinse strawberries and remove stems. Cut each strawberry into 3 or 4 thick slices. Add to bananas and pineapple.
5. Rinse grapes and cut each one in half. Add to other fruit.
6. Rinse blueberries and add to fruit, mixing gently.
7. Into a small cup, measure 2 tablespoons pineapple juice. (Drink the rest). Add coconut syrup or honey and stir carefully until it's blended. Pour over fruit and mix well. Makes 6 to 8 servings.

color
waihooluu

loose gown
muumuu

sit
noho

Carl
Kala

Agnes
Akeneki

Jane
Kini

six
eono

rainbow
ānuenue

71

BAKED APPLE DELUXE

6 large baking apples
1 can (8¼ oz.) Dole Crushed
   Pineapple
¼ cup chopped pecans
   Hot water
½ cup dark brown sugar,
   firmly packed
1 teaspoon ground cinnamon

1. Turn on oven to 350° F.
2. Ask someone who knows to help you core the apples.
3. Arrange apples in baking dish.
4. Open pineapple with can opener. Hold a strainer over a small bowl. Empty can into strainer and let syrup drain off into bowl.
5. Combine chopped nuts and pineapple. Spoon this into the centers of apples, forcing it down with clean fingers.
6. Measure syrup from pineapple. Add enough hot water to make ½ cup. Stir in brown sugar and cinnamon until sugar dissolves. Carefully pour this over apples in dish.
7. Place in oven and bake for about an hour.
8. With potholders, remove from oven. Turn oven off. Makes 6 servings.

Theodore
Keokolo

tiny
pālanaīki

carry on the back
e waha

good luck
pōmaika'i

apple
apala

heavy
kaumaha

tomorrow
apōpō

PINEAPPLE CLOUD DESSERT

1 can (8¼ oz.) Dole Crushed
    Pineapple
1 tablespoon unflavored gelatin
1 cup cooked rice
¼ cup powdered sugar
⅓ cup toasted almonds*
1 half-pint whipping cream
1 teaspoon vanilla extract
2 tablespoons sugar

1. Open pineapple with a can opener. Hold a large strainer over a small saucepan and pour pineapple into strainer. Let all the syrup drain into the pan.
2. Set strainer with pineapple aside. Sprinkle unflavored gelatin over syrup in pan.
3. Cook over medium heat, stirring with a spoon, until syrup just starts to boil.
4. Remove pan from heat and stir in crushed pineapple, rice, powdered sugar and toasted almonds.
5. Cover pan and place in refrigerator for about half an hour.
6. Pour cream and vanilla into a mixing bowl. Whip with electric mixer at medium speed until it gets foamy. Add sugar a little at a time, keeping mixer on. Stop the mixer when the whipped cream is stiff.
7. Fold the pineapple mixture into the whipped cream.
8. Spoon the dessert into pretty dishes. Chill in refrigerator for at least an hour. Makes 6 servings.

*To toast almonds, place on a baking sheet in an even layer and bake in a 400° F oven for 10 to 15 minutes.

cloud
ao

rice
laiki

Angela
Anakela

Rebecca
Lepeka

be careful
mālama pono

drip
kulu

sweet
momona

READY-SET-GO! DESSERT

2 large Dole Bananas
1 can (1 lb. 4 oz.) Dole
   Chunk Pineapple
1 cup miniature marshmallows
¼ cup maraschino cherries
2 tablespoons flaked coconut

1. Peel bananas and cut into ¼-inch slices. Place banana slices in medium-size bowl.
2. Open pineapple with a can-opener. Add pineapple chunks and all the syrup to bananas.
3. Measure marshmallows into the bowl.
4. With a small knife, cut each cherry in half; add to fruit.
5. Mix all together. Sprinkle coconut on top.
6. Cover bowl with plastic wrap and place in refrigerator for about an hour. Makes 6 servings.

go
hele

John
Keoni

Bonnie
Poni

laugh
akaaka

lake
loko nui

beautiful water
wainani

pond
loko i'a

CHOCOLATE PARFAITS

2 cups milk
1 package (4½ oz.) chocolate-
flavored instant pudding mix
1 cup granola cereal
2 large Dole Bananas
6 maraschino cherries

1. Pour milk into a medium-size mixer bowl; add instant pudding mix. With electric mixer on low speed, blend pudding mixture for 2 minutes. Scrape sides of bowl and beater.
2. Place about two spoonfuls of pudding in each of 6 serving glasses.
3. Sprinkle one teaspoonful of granola into each glass.
4. Peel banana and cut into ¼-inch slices. Arrange slices on top of granola in each glass.
5. Spoon the rest of the pudding on top of bananas.
6. Peel the other banana and cut into ¼-inch slices. Arrange slices on pudding.
7. Sprinkle remaining granola over bananas.
8. Top each parfait with a maraschino cherry. Makes 6 servings.

Rachel
Lahela

strike up the music
kanikapila

darling
ipo

friendly
ho alohaloha

entertain
hookipa

outside
mawaho

spring
puna

79

PROOF-OF-THE-PUDDING

⅓ cup sugar
3 tablespoons cornstarch
¼ teaspoon salt
2 cups milk
1 egg
2 tablespoons butter

1 teaspoon vanilla extract
3 drops yellow food coloring
2 large Dole bananas
2 tablespoons sliced almonds
  or coconut

1. Measure sugar, cornstarch and salt into a medium-size saucepan; mix together with a wooden spoon. Slowly add milk, stirring constantly, until smooth.
2. Place over medium heat and stir slowly until mixture boils and thickens. Remove from heat. Turn heat off.
3. In a small bowl, beat egg slightly with a fork. Add a spoonful of hot pudding to egg and blend well. Then add egg to pudding mixture, stirring well.
4. Add butter, vanilla and food coloring to pudding, stir until butter melts. Place piece of waxed paper on top of pudding and let cool.
5. Peel bananas and cut into ¼-inch slices; gently mix into pudding. Pour into a serving bowl. Sprinkle with almonds or coconut on top. Makes 4 to 6 servings.

pudding
pūkini

Howard
Haoa

coconut
niu

always
mau

down
i lalo

bark
ili lāau

high
kiekie

climb
pii

AMERICANA BANANA PIE

½ package (11 oz.)
   pie crust mix
2 tablespoons water
2 cups milk

1 package (4 oz.) vanilla flavored
   instant pudding mix
3 large Dole Bananas
2 cups frozen whipped topping, thawed

1. Place oven rack in center of oven. Turn oven to 450° F.
2. Measure pie crust mix into a small bowl. Add water and mix with a fork until pastry holds together.
3. With your hands, shape pastry into a ball.
4. Tear off 2 sheets of waxed paper about 12 inches long. Place one sheet on a flat surface. Put ball of pastry on waxed paper. Cover with second sheet of waxed paper.
5. Using a rolling pin, lightly roll out pastry into a 10-inch circle.
6. Carefully remove top sheet of waxed paper. Turn pastry over into an 8-inch pie plate. Then remove the second sheet of waxed paper.
7. Gently press edges of pastry onto pie plate. Trim or flute edges.
8. Prick crust with a fork all over.
9. Place in oven and bake for 12 minutes. With potholders, remove pie crust from oven and let cool. Turn oven off.
10. Measure milk into a medium-size mixer bowl. Add pudding mix. With electric mixer on low speed, blend pudding mixture for 2 minutes.
11. Peel bananas and cut into ¼-inch slices; add to pudding. Gently mix bananas into pudding with a wooden spoon.
12. Spoon banana pudding into cooled pie crust.
13. Place in refrigerator for 2 hours to let filling set.
14. Spread whipped topping over pie to serve. Makes 8 to 10 servings.

Rose
Loke

small guitar
ukulele

joy
hauoli

Daniel
Kaniela

heart
pu'uwai

happy
hau'oli

sing
hīmeni

LUNCH BOX COOKIES

½ cup butter, softened	2 large Dole bananas
1 cup brown sugar, firmly packed	1 cup flour
	1 teaspoon salt
½ cup granulated sugar	1 teaspoon baking powder
1 egg	2½ cups rolled oats
1 teaspoon vanilla	1 cup chocolate chips

1. If butter is cold, let it stand at room temperature for 1 hour to soften.
2. Place oven rack in center of oven. Turn oven to 375° F. Lightly grease 2 cookie sheets with about 1 tablespoon shortening each.
3. Measure brown sugar, granulated sugar, and butter into medium-size mixer bowl. With electric mixer at low speed, stir sugar and butter until it sticks together. Then turn up the mixer to medium speed and beat until the mixture looks creamy.
4. Add egg and vanilla; beat on medium speed until fluffy.
5. Peel bananas; break into pieces and place in a small bowl. With a fork, mash bananas; then add to sugar mixture. Beat at medium speed for one minute.
6. In a separate small bowl, stir together flour, salt and baking powder; then add to sugar mixture, blending on slow speed.
7. Stir in oats, one cup at a time, and chocolate chips. Scrape beaters.
8. Place teaspoonfuls of dough about 3 inches apart on greased cookie sheets.
9. Place filled cookie sheets in oven and bake for 20 minutes.
10. With potholders, remove cookie sheets from oven. Lift cookies with a spatula onto wire racks to cool.
11. Refill cookie sheets with spoonfuls of dough and bake as before. When all cookies are baked, turn oven off. Makes about 4½ dozen cookies.

Deborah
Kepola

talk
walaau

friend
aikāne

fun
le'ale'a

share
māhele

doll
kii

feed
hānai

CHARLIE'S SPECIAL SUNDAE

2 large Dole Bananas
½ cup chunky-style peanut butter
¼ cup dark corn syrup
Vanilla ice cream
Chocolate chips

1. Peel bananas; break into pieces and place in a medium-size bowl. Mash bananas with a fork.
2. Measure peanut butter and corn syrup into bowl; using a wire whip, mix well with bananas. Set aside.
3. Scoop vanilla ice cream into serving dishes. Top with banana sauce. Sprinkle chocolate chips over all.
4. This makes enough sauce for about 8 servings. If you don't use it all at once, spoon sauce into a jar or plastic container; cover and keep in the refrigerator.

Charles
Kale

hat
pāpale

finish
pau

I
Owau

weave
ulana

almost
aneane loa

name
inoa

87

SPICY POUNDCAKE

1 package (17 oz.) poundcake mix
½ teaspoon ground cinnamon
¼ teaspoon ground nutmeg
¼ cup milk
1 large ripe Dole Banana
¼ cup plain yogurt
2 eggs

1. Place oven rack in center of oven. Turn oven to 325° F.
2. Grease a 9-inch loaf pan, using about 1 tablespoon shortening.
3. Empty poundcake mix into a medium-size mixer bowl. Add cinnamon, nutmeg and milk. With electric mixer on low speed, blend mixture 1 minute.
4. Peel banana; break into pieces and place in a small bowl. Mash banana with a fork; then add to poundcake batter with yogurt and eggs.
5. Beat at medium speed for 1 minute.
6. Pour batter into greased pan. Place on rack in oven and bake for 1 hour and 15 minutes.
7. With potholders, remove cake from oven. Turn oven off.
8. Place pan on rack to cool 10 minutes, then turn pan upside down on the rack and remove pan from cake. Let cake cool completely before serving. Makes 8 to 10 servings.

Roger
 Lōkela

pound
 paona

cake
 mea'ono

taro
 kalo

work
 hana

tired
 luhi

surprise
 pūiwa

89

BANANA FUDGE BROWNIES

1 package (15½ oz.) brownie mix
1 egg
½ cup water
3 large Dole bananas
1 cup whipping cream
2 tablespoons sugar

1. Place oven rack in center of oven. Turn oven to 350° F.
2. Grease an 8-inch square baking pan with about 1 tablespoon shortening.
3. Empty brownie mix into a medium-size mixing bowl. Add egg and water.
4. Peel one banana; break it into pieces and place in a separate small bowl. With a fork, mash banana. Add mashed banana to brownie mix.
5. With a large spoon, mix batter until it is smooth.
6. Spread batter in the greased baking pan. Carefully place in oven in center of rack. Bake for 30 minutes.
7. With potholders, remove brownies from oven. Let cool. Turn oven off.
8. While brownies are cooling, pour whipping cream into a small mixing bowl. Whip at medium speed with electric mixer until soft peaks form when you lift the beaters. Sprinkle sugar over cream. Then continue beating just until stiff peaks form.
9. Cover bowl with plastic wrap and place in refrigerator until you are ready to serve.
10. Cut cooled brownies into squares.
11. When ready to serve, peel the other two bananas and cut into ½-inch slices. Place brownies on serving plate, spoon whipped cream over top and arrange banana slices on whipped cream. Makes 16 servings.

Caroline
Kalolaina

smile
minoaka

pour
ninini

prepare
hoomākaukau

imagine
kuhi

best love to you
aloha nui oe

sunshine
pāana a ka lā

INDEX

DRINKS (continued)

SALADS

SANDWICHES

PAU!
All Finished!

Kipa hou mai!
Come Again!

ALOHA!
Farewell!